T0067654

First published 2010 by North Parade Publishing Ltd.

First Racehorse for Young Readers Edition 2017

All rights to any and all materials in copyright owned by the publisher are strictly reserved by the publisher.

Racehorse for Young Readers books may be purchased in bulk at special discounts for sales promotion, corporate gifts, fund-raising, or educational purposes. Special editions can also be created to specifications. For details, contact the Special Sales Department, Skyhorse Publishing, 307 West 36th Street, 11th Floor, New York, NY 10018 or info@skyhorsepublishing.com.

Racehorse for Young Readers™ is a pending trademark of Skyhorse Publishing, Inc.®,
a Delaware corporation.

Visit our website at www.skyhorsepublishing.com.

10 9 8 7 6 5 4 3 2

Cover design by North Parade Publishing
Predominant artwork and imagery: Shutterstock

ISBN: 978-1-63158-241-7

Printed in China

My First 1000 Words

FOR YOUNG READERS

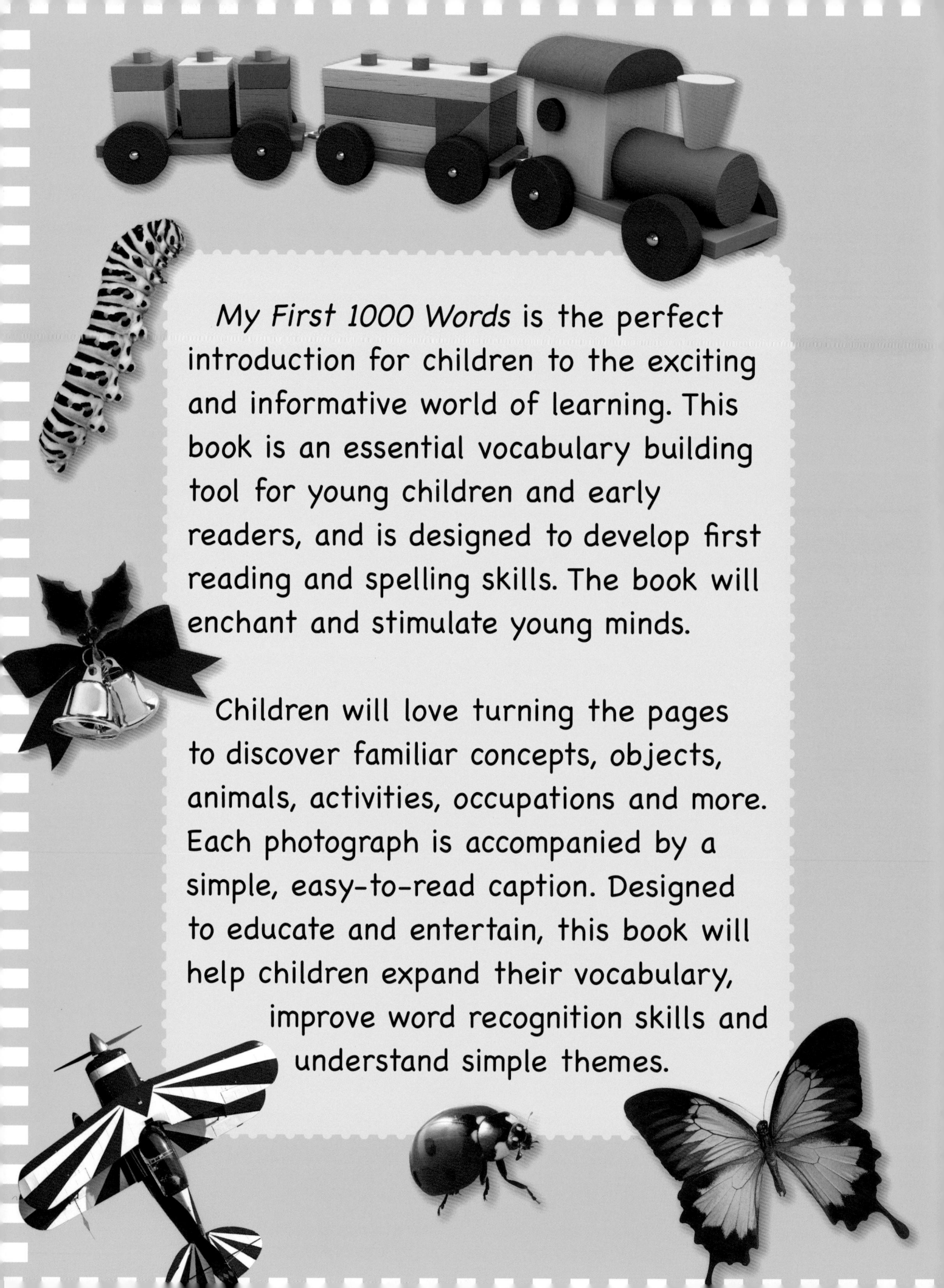

My First 1000 Words is the perfect introduction for children to the exciting and informative world of learning. This book is an essential vocabulary building tool for young children and early readers, and is designed to develop first reading and spelling skills. The book will enchant and stimulate young minds.

Children will love turning the pages to discover familiar concepts, objects, animals, activities, occupations and more. Each photograph is accompanied by a simple, easy-to-read caption. Designed to educate and entertain, this book will help children expand their vocabulary, improve word recognition skills and understand simple themes.

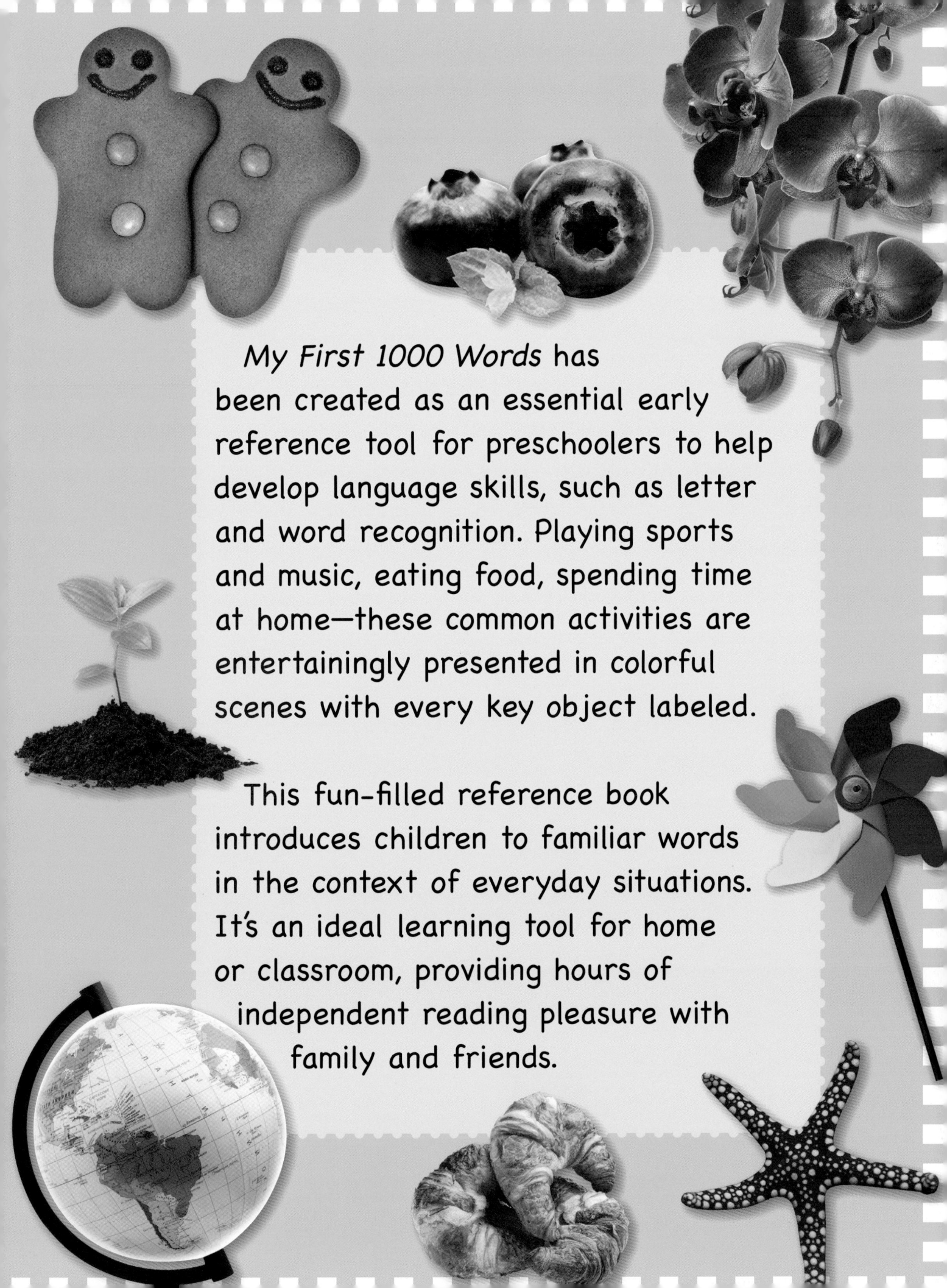

My First 1000 Words has been created as an essential early reference tool for preschoolers to help develop language skills, such as letter and word recognition. Playing sports and music, eating food, spending time at home—these common activities are entertainingly presented in colorful scenes with every key object labeled.

This fun-filled reference book introduces children to familiar words in the context of everyday situations. It's an ideal learning tool for home or classroom, providing hours of independent reading pleasure with family and friends.

Household Pets

These animals are found at home. Do you have any pets?

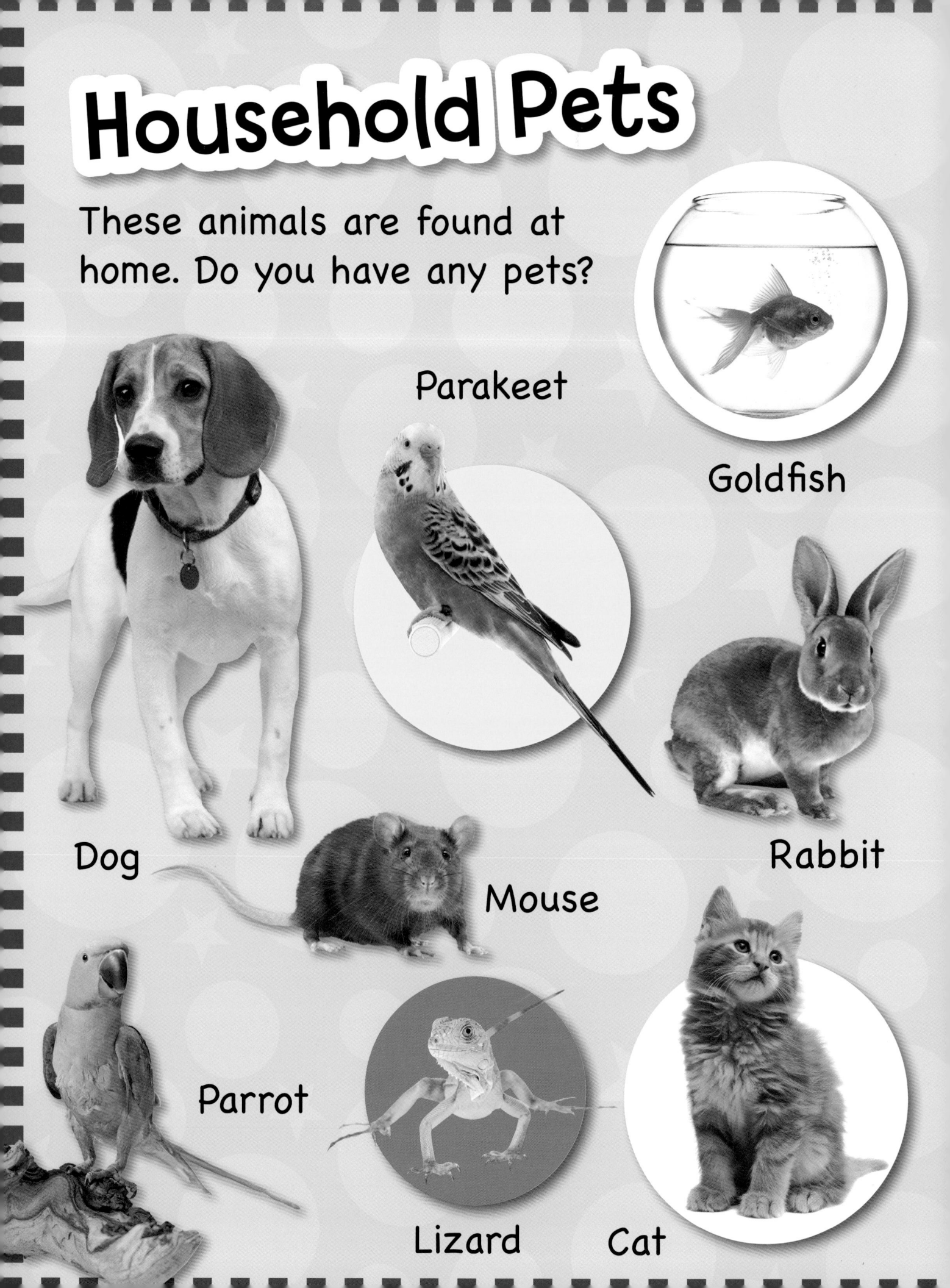

Farm Animals

These animals live and work on and around farms and parks.

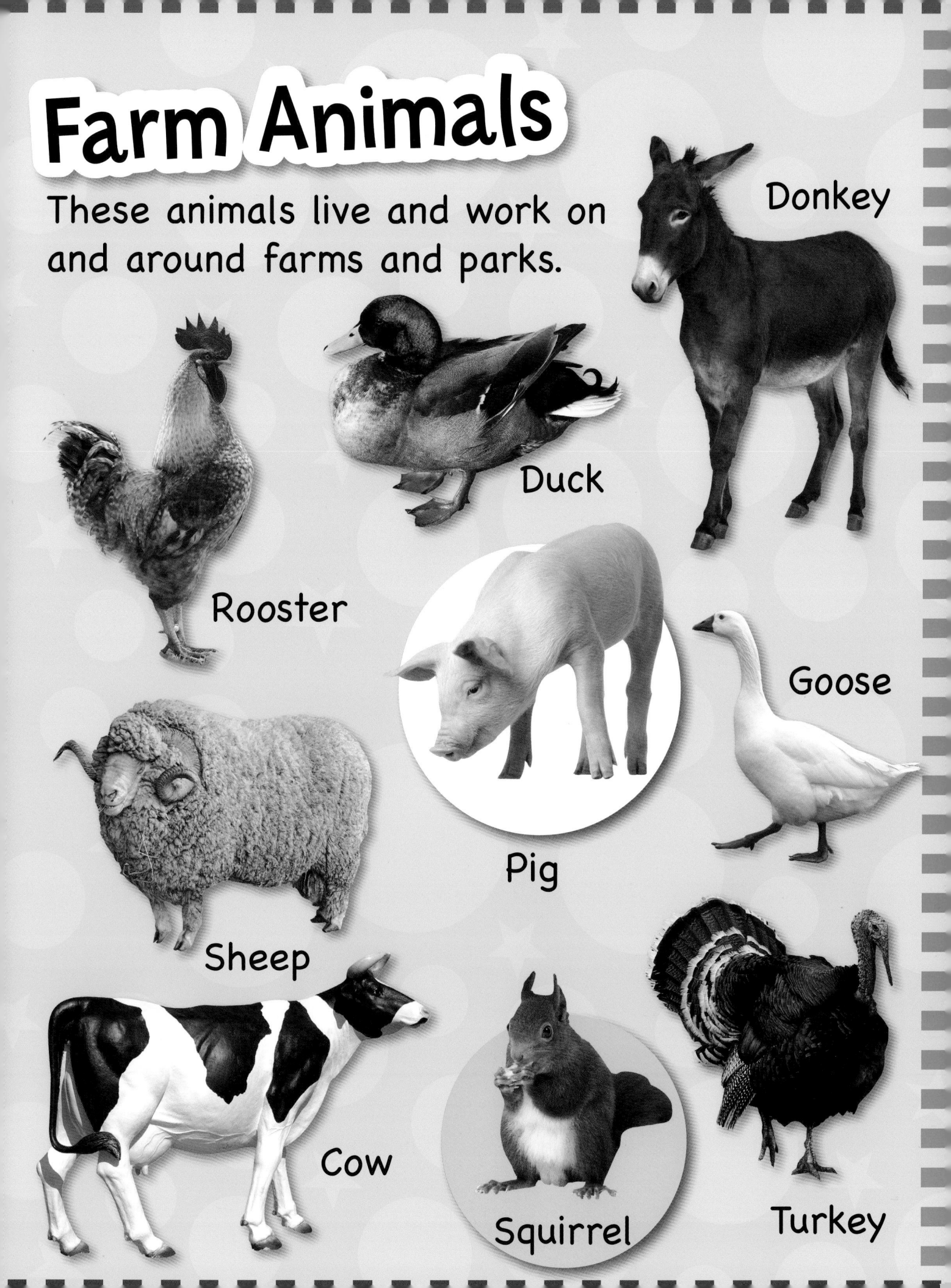

In the Garden

How many of these creatures have you seen in your garden?

Ladybird
Centipede
Wasp
Moth
Grasshopper
Snail
Slug
Magpie
Green Cricket
Earthworm

In the Jungle

These are some of the wild animals that live in or near jungles.

Monkey
Toucan
Spider Monkey
Orangutan
Macaw
Bat
Warthog
Capybara
Howler Monkey
Leopard

On the Grasslands

Some animals live on the grasslands. Let's take a look at them.

In the Mountains

The mountains are also home to several animals. Let's see what they are.

In the Pond

Have you looked into a pond? Did you see any of these creatures?

Frog

Dragon Fly

Tadpole

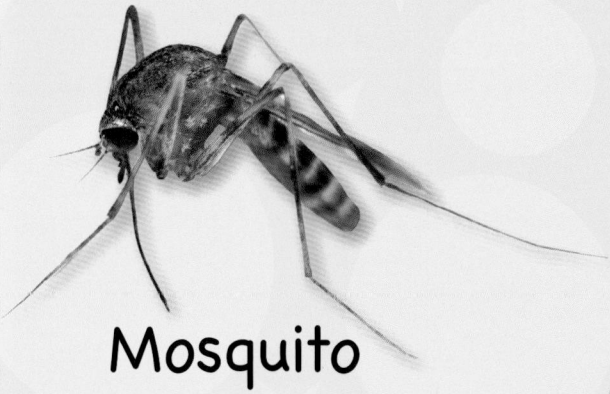

Mosquito

Koi Fish

Salamander

May Fly

Water Strider

Toad

In the Deserts

Animals can also be found in the deserts. Here are some of them.

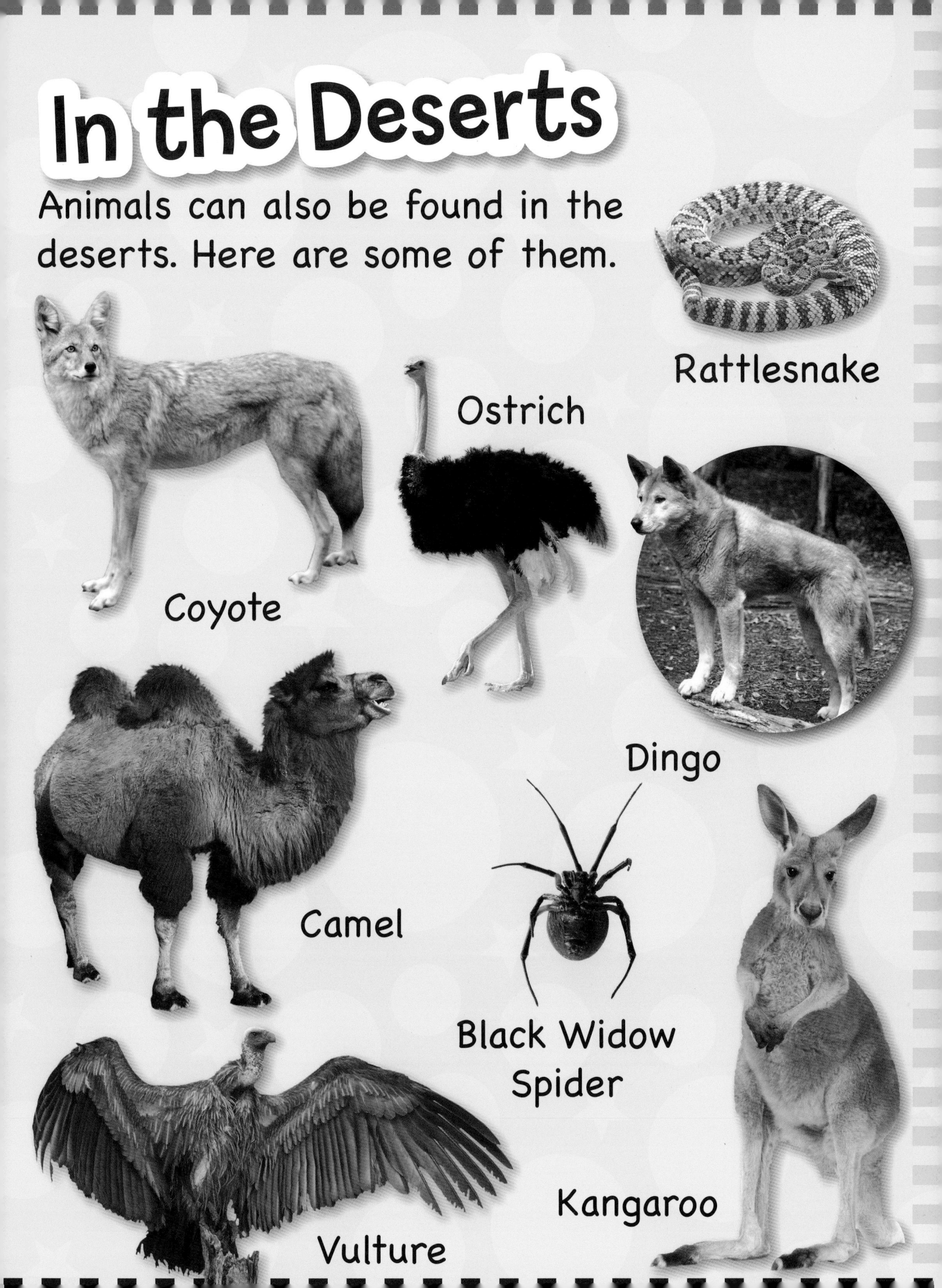

In the Oceans

The seas are home to many creatures as well as fish.

Dolphin

Sponge

Angel Fish

Star Fish

Sting Ray

Coral

Pelican

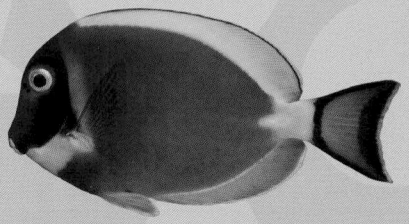

Parrot Fish

Killer Whale
Humpback Whale
Clownfish
Seahorse
Seagull
Eel
Crab
Octopus
Great White Shark

In the Rivers

Even the rivers are teeming with wildlife and not all of them are fish.

At the Poles

These creatures live in the extreme cold of the poles.

Good Morning

What do you do when you get up in the morning?

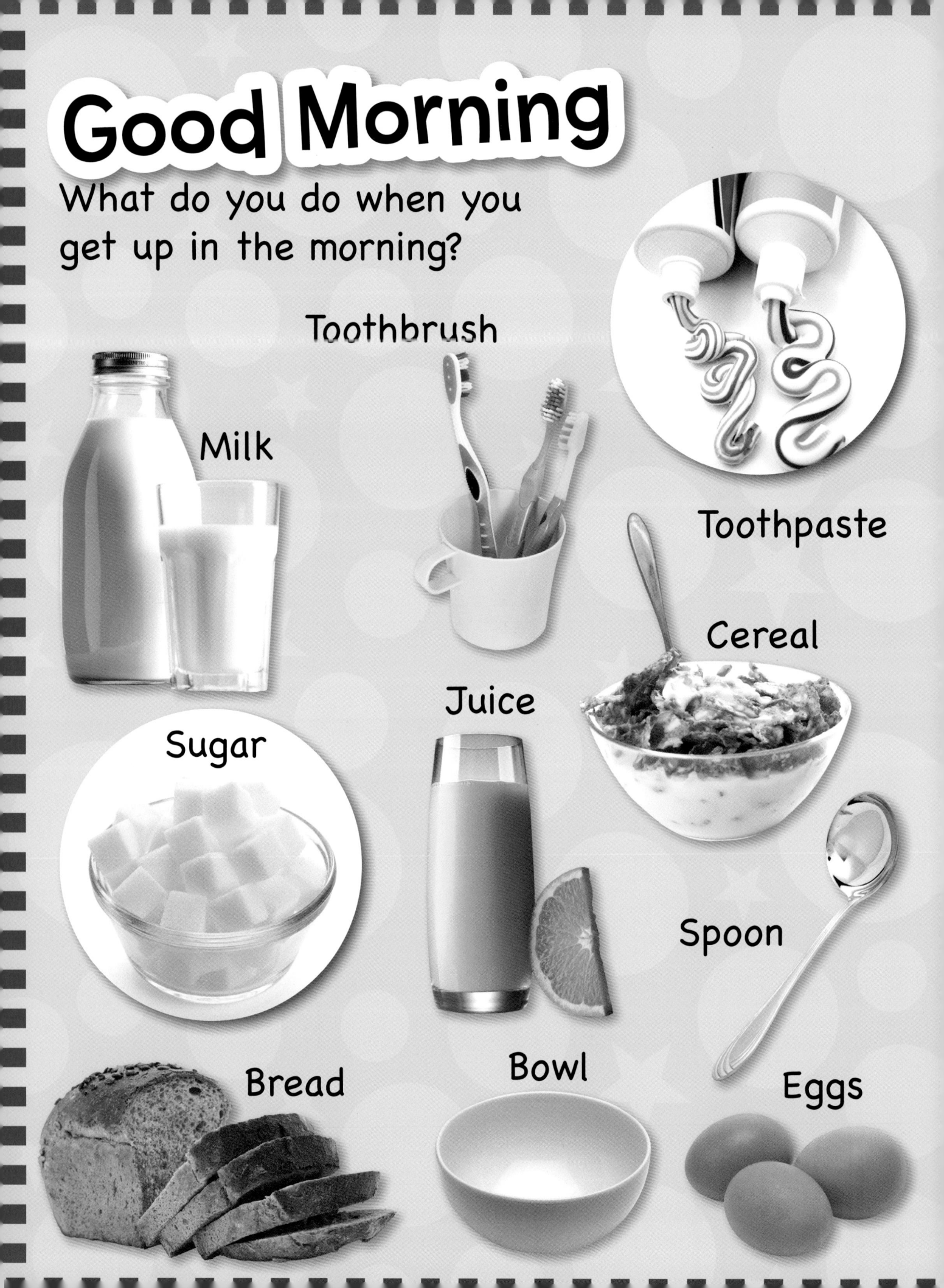

Time for a Bath

After brushing your teeth and having breakast, it's time for a bath.

My Body

These are the different important parts of your body.

Feet
Hair
Toes
Eye
Nose
Fingers
Teeth
Arm
Ear

What I Do

How many of these activities do you do everyday?

My Clothes

These are the different types of clothes you wear everyday.

Around the House

These are some objects around the house. Can you name them?

Radio
Key
Window
Music
Music Player
Sofa
Air Conditioner
Fan
Timer
Roof
Picture

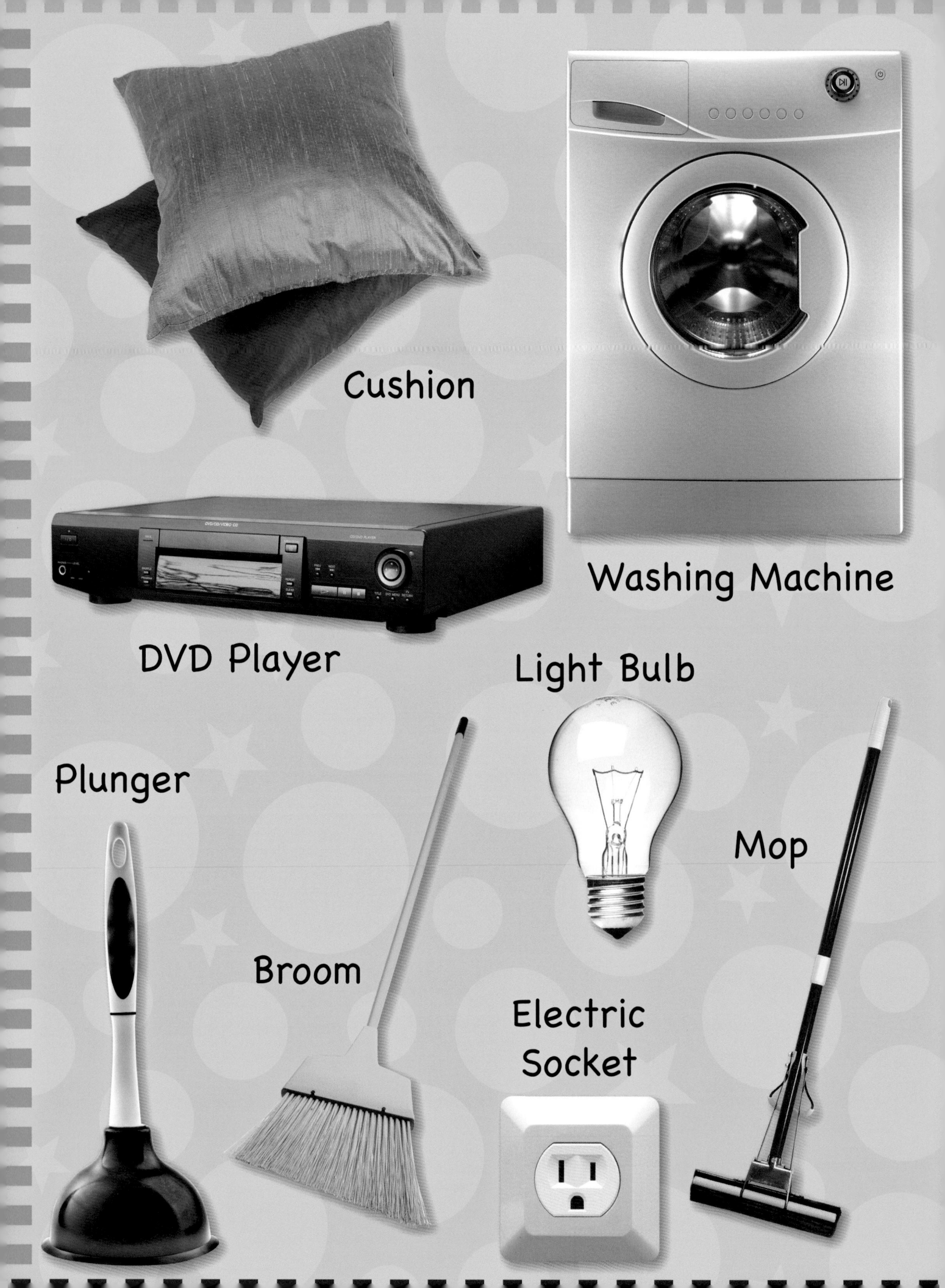
Cushion
Washing Machine
DVD Player
Light Bulb
Plunger
Mop
Broom
Electric
Socket

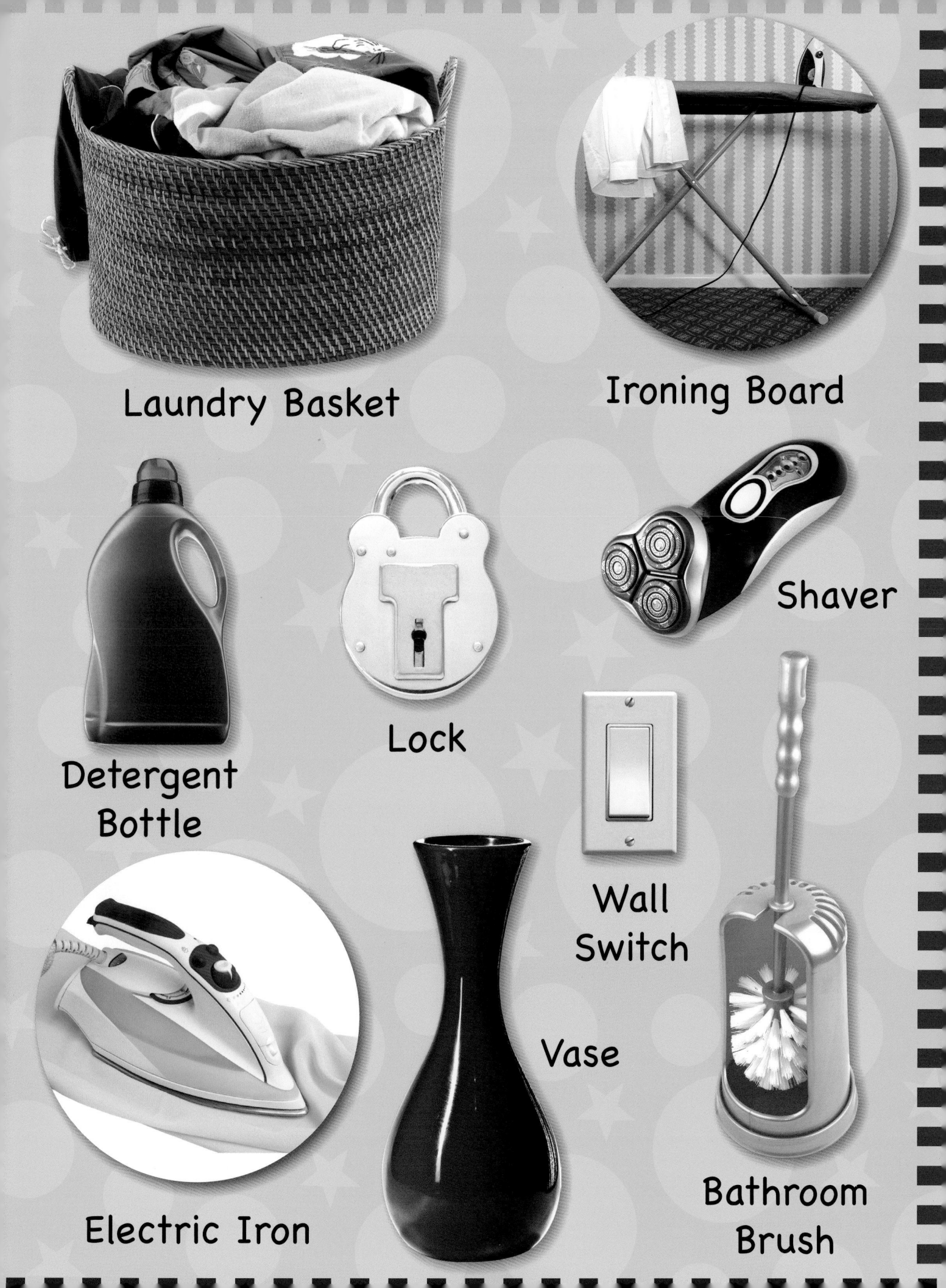
Laundry Basket
Ironing Board
Detergent Bottle
Lock
Shaver
Wall Switch
Electric Iron
Vase
Bathroom Brush

Doghouse
Birdhouse
Fire Extinguisher
Coaster
Umbrella Stand
Toolbox
Rolodex

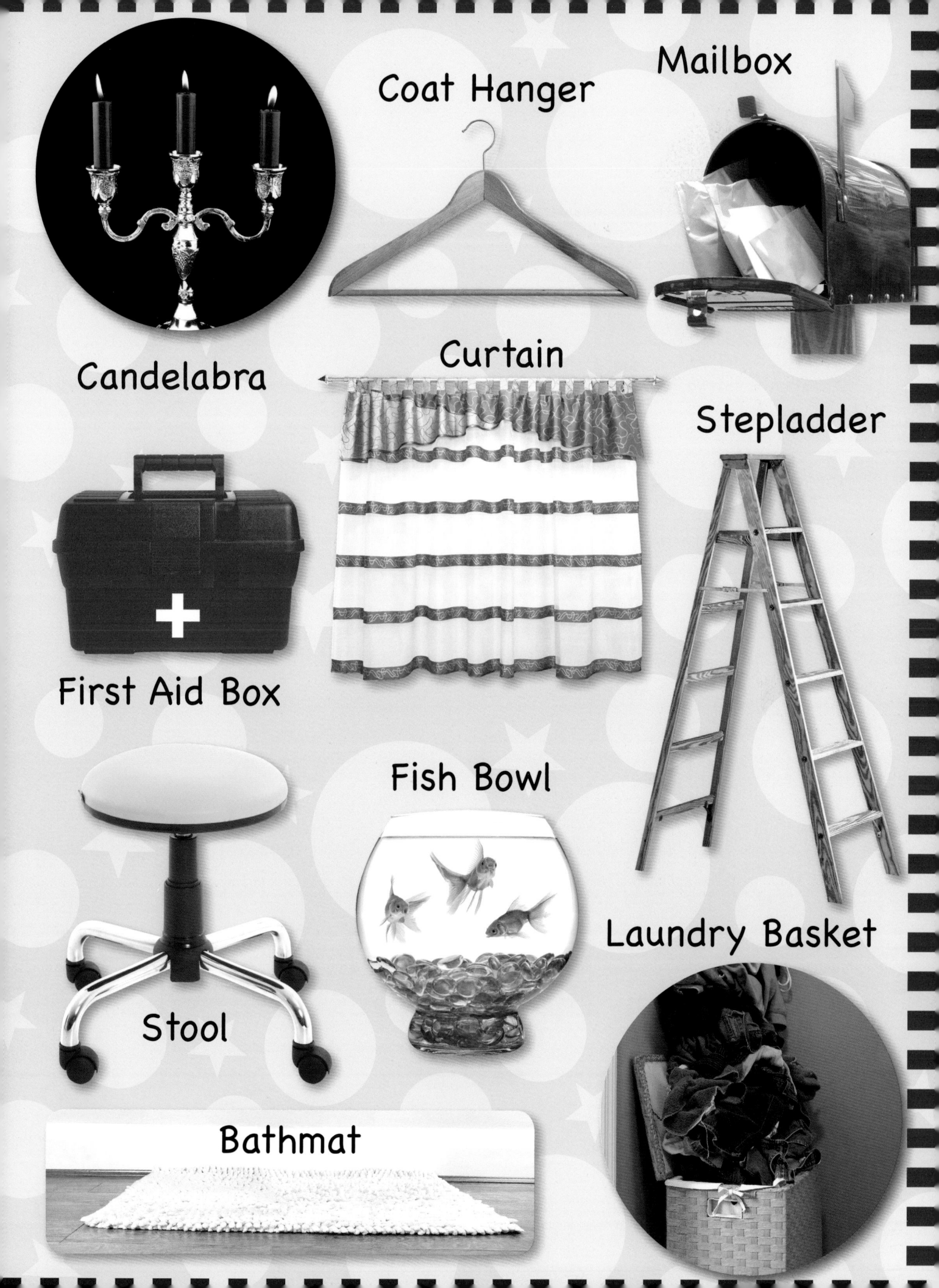
Coat Hanger
Mailbox
Candelabra
Curtain
Stepladder
First Aid Box
Fish Bowl
Laundry Basket
Stool
Bathmat

It's Bedtime

It's time for bed. Do you recognize these objects?

Pillow

Bed

Pajamas

Night Light

Blanket

Soft Toy

Reading Lamp

Books

Colors

How many of these colors do you recognize?

Green Apple

Orange

Violet Flower

Yellow Flower

Red Purse

Black Hat

Blue Butterfly

Gray Bag

Purple Eggplant

Let's Play

Which of these toys would you like to play with?

Toy Plane
Robot
Ball
Toy Phone
Toy Blocks
Wagon
Rocking Horse
Doll
Car

Getting Ready

Going on a trip? Let's get ready for it first.

Backpack

Map

Tickets

Passport

Suitcase

Compass

What to Pack

Let's see, what do you need to pack for the trip?

At the Beach

Aren't beaches fun? Have you spotted any of these objects on a beach?

Frisbee
Seashell
Coral
Dolphin
Life Buoy
Beach Umbrella
Deck Chair
Crab
Beach Shovel

Christmas

Yay, it's Christmas time!
Time for some holiday cheer.

Christmas Stocking
Cookies
Stars
Sleigh
Nativity
Holly
Holly Wreath
Tinsel
Reindeer

Cracker
Fireplace
Christmas Hat
Mistletoe
Gingerbread Men
Merry Christmas!
and Happy New Year!
Red Ribbon
Christmas Card
Candy Cane
Christmas Tree
Carol Singers

Snowman
Eggnog
Christmas Decorations
Elf
Lights
Family
Chimney

Halloween

Shhh . . . it's halloween. All the ghosts and spirits are about.

Candy

Scarecrow

Costumes

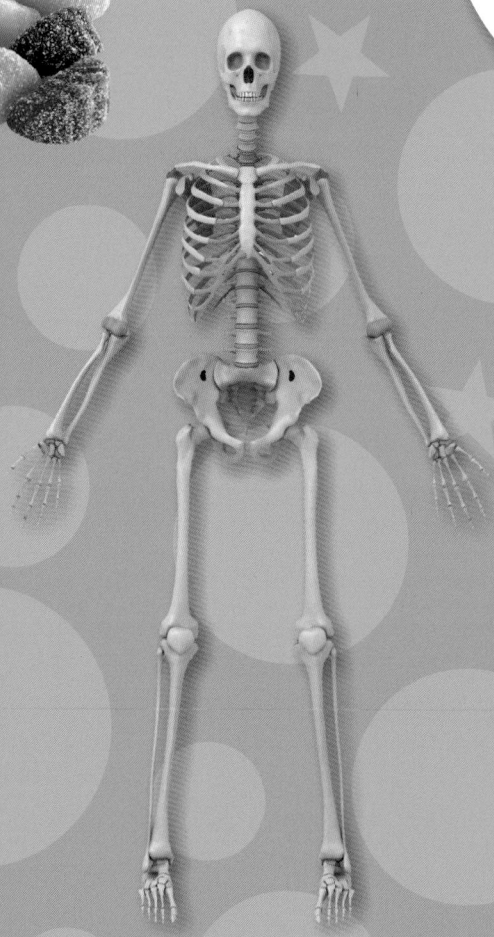

Skeleton

Bonfire

Ghost

Pumpkin Pie

Broomstick
Candle
Vampire
Bat
Mummy
Fireworks
Autumn Leaves
Witch
Pumpkin

Easter

Easter is not just about the egg hunt, is it?

Jelly Beans

Chocolate

Basket

Easter Eggs

Easter Bunny

Chick

Bonnet

Day Out

How about a day of fun out with the other kids?

Swimming Pool

Binoculars

Pinecone

Treehouse

Tent

Camera

Windmill

Pebbles

Amusement Park

Thrilling rides make a great day at the amusement park.

Toy Car

Carousel

Sky Balloon Ride

Swings

Skee-Ball

Go-Kart

Roller Coaster
Boat Ride
Whirligig
Water Slide
Bumper Car
TICKETS
Ticket Booth
Spring Horse
Kiddie Train
Cotton Candy
Ferris Wheel

In the Kitchen

How many of these objects have you seen in your kitchen?

Frying Pan
Food Containers
Kitchen Scales
Knife
Baking Tray
Rolling Pin
Cutting Board
Dishwasher
Juicer
Ladle

In the Office

The office is where people do their work.

Pen Stand
Pen
Armchair
Hole Punch
Notebook
Bookshelf
Box File
Stapler

In the Dining Room

You may find all these objects in the room where you have your meals.

Place Mat
Plate
Yogurt
Soup Bowl
Salt and
Pepper Shakers
Glass
Napkin
Ring
Napkin
Holder
Napkin

In the Garden

Do you have a garden? Have you seen these objects there before?

Shovel
Clippers
Rake
Paving Stones
Spade
Flower
Tree
Trowel
Fertilizer
Weeds

Early Vehicles

These are some of the earliest forms of transport used by man.

Longboat

Sedan Chair

Stagecoach

Galley

Buckboard

Buggy

Covered Wagon

Horse-Drawn Cab

Two-Wheelers

The bicycle is not the only machine on two wheels.

Cars

There are so many different types of cars.

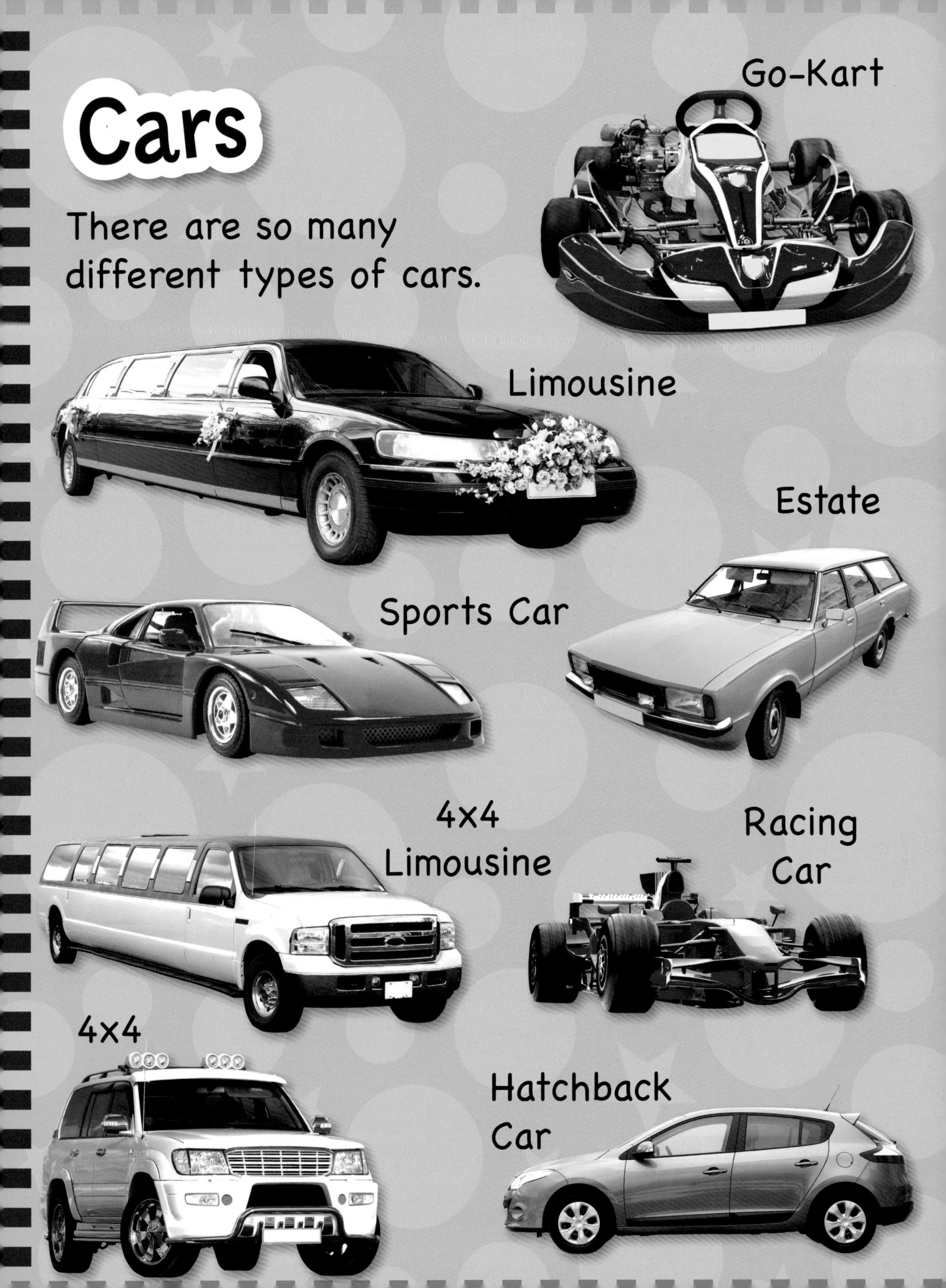

Convertible
Dragster
Saloon
Golf Cart
Vintage Car
Mini Car
Dune Buggy
Minibus
Jeep

Working Machines

These machines are used to do different types of work.

Farm Tractor

Combine Harvester

Steamroller

Taxi

Bulldozer

Forklift

Ambulance

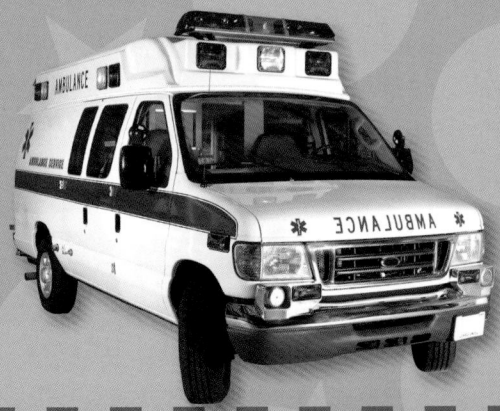

Rock Grader

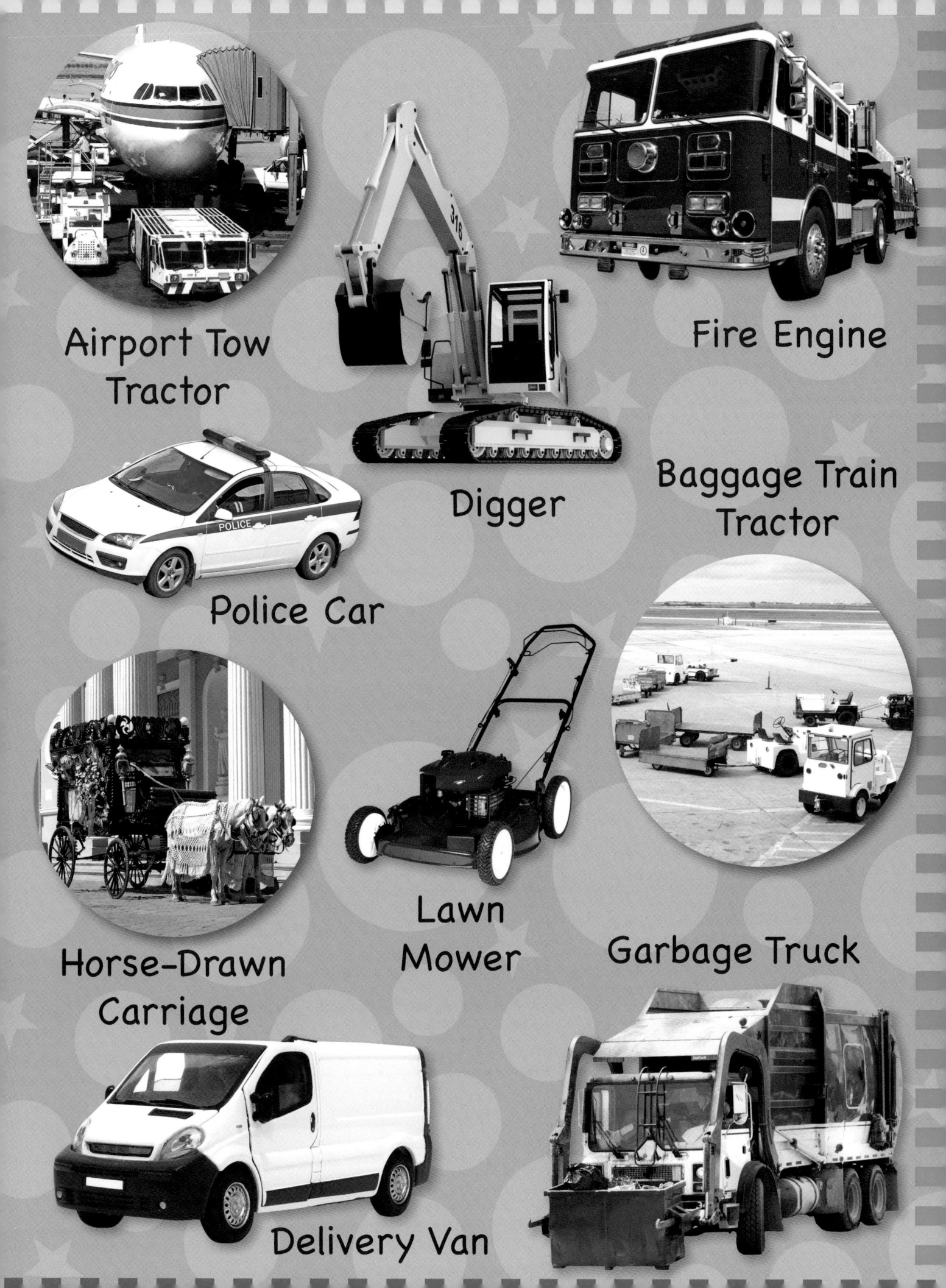
Airport Tow Tractor
Fire Engine
Digger
Baggage Train Tractor
POLICE
Police Car
Horse-Drawn Carriage
Lawn Mower
Garbage Truck
Delivery Van

Trucks & Buses

Have you ever seen so many different kinds of trucks and buses?

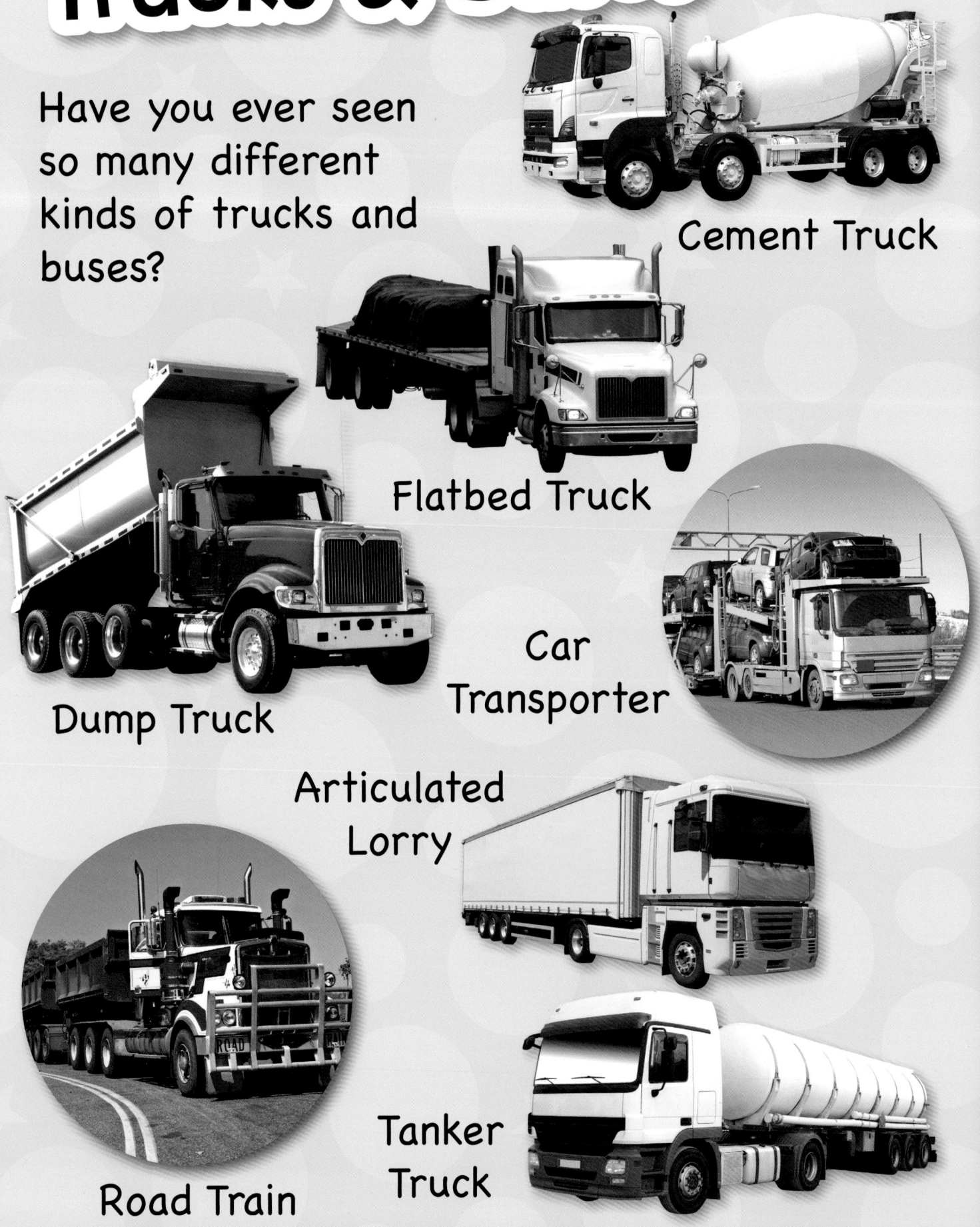

Tow Truck
Mining Truck
Bus
Motor Home
Pickup Truck
Monster Truck
Mini Truck
Trailer Truck
Double-Decker Bus
15
TRAFALGAR SQUARE
Delivery Truck

Watercrafts

All these machines move on or below the water.

Hovercraft

Cruise Ship

Kayak

Cargo Ship

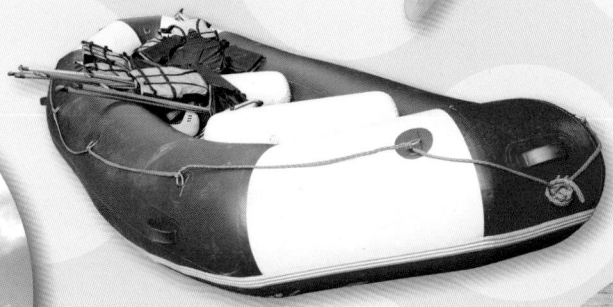

Life Raft

Barge

Canoe

Tanker Ship
Rowboat
Submarine
Motorboat
Race Boat
Sailboard
Luxury Boat
Catamaran
Sailboat
Hydrofoil

Aircrafts

High in the sky, that is where you will find these machines.

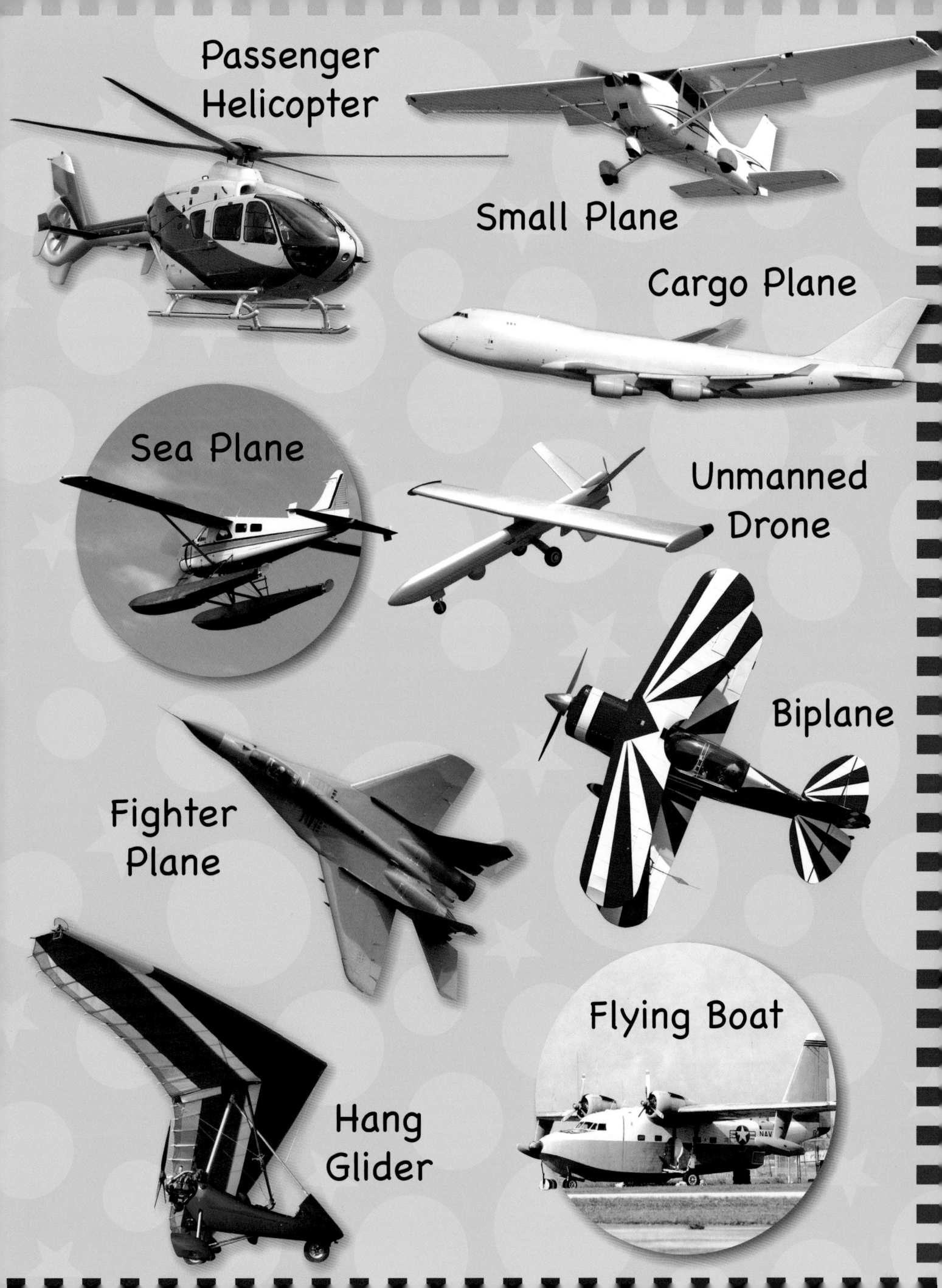
Passenger Helicopter
Small Plane
Cargo Plane
Sea Plane
Unmanned Drone
Biplane
Fighter Plane
Flying Boat
Hang Glider

Other Vehicles

These machines are all different from the others. Can you tell why?

Stroller
Amphibious Vehicle
Monorail
Skateboard
Scooter
Quad
Sled
Rocket
Tram
Jet Ski

How I Feel

We all have feelings and express them all the time.

Lonely
Playful
Sad
Angry
Scared
Tired
Teary
Hurt
Scowl

Musical Instruments

Everybody loves music. Listening to music is a soothing experience.

Saxophone
Maracas
Clarinet
Violin
Acoustic Guitar
Banjo
Piano
Ocarina
Carved African Djembe

Sports

Playing a sport is not just fun, it is also good for your health.

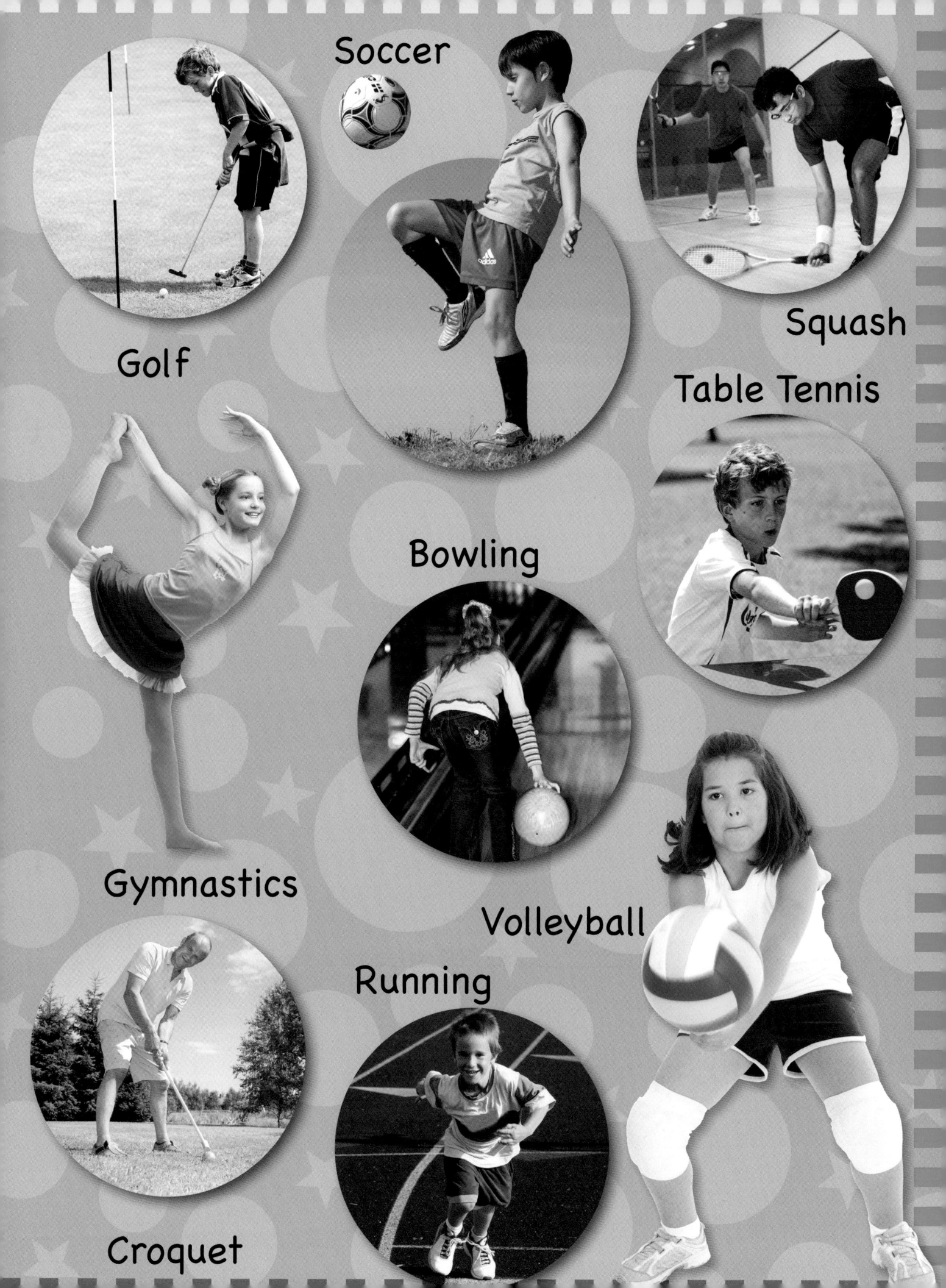
Soccer
Golf
Squash
Table Tennis
Bowling
Gymnastics
Volleyball
Running
Croquet

Games We Play

And now it's time for some fun and games with friends.

Skipping

Follow the Leader

Patty-Cake

Backgammon

Cowboys and Indians

Checkers

Jigsaw Puzzles

Hopscotch
Chess
Hide-and-Seek
Frisbee
Rock, Paper, Scissors
Tag
Tic-Tac-Toe
Marbles
Leapfrog
Catch

Descriptive Words

These words tell you what something looks or feels like.

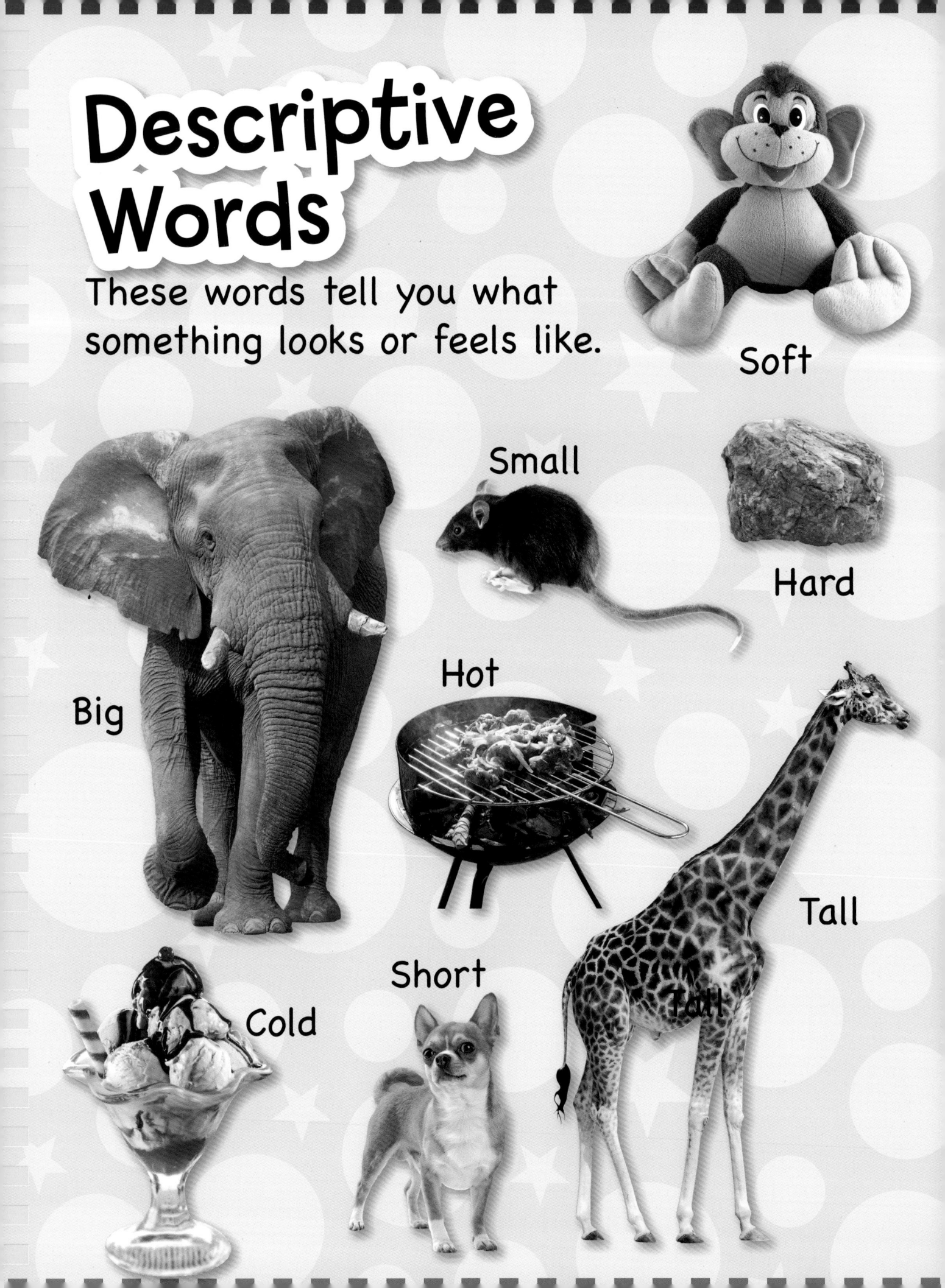

Straight

Wide

Narrow

Bright

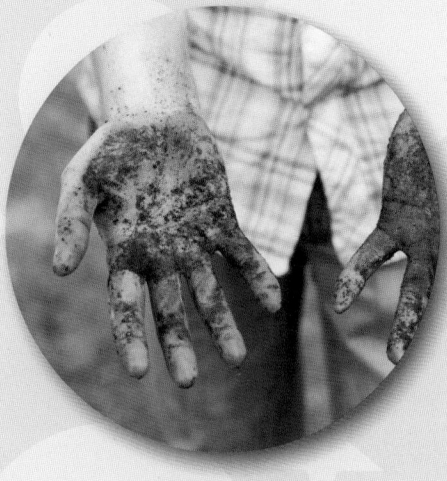

Dirty

Weak

Strong

Thin

Fat

In the School

These objects you may find in your school.

Cafeteria

Locker

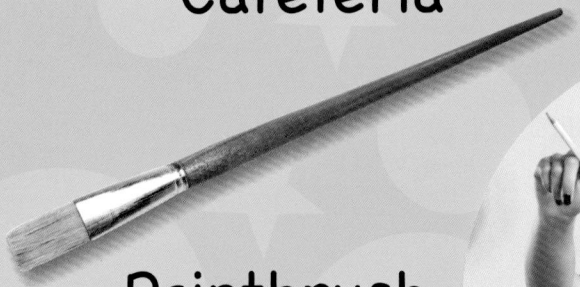

Paintbrush

Teacher

Schooldesk

Schoolbag

Flipchart
Lunch Box
Trash Can
Notice Board
Notebook
Social Studies & Government
The Natural Sciences
Spelling
Literature
Mathematics
Textbooks
Water Bottle
Globe
Chalk
Blackboard

Clothing Accessories

Accessories are used with clothes and help us look good.

Bow Tie
Hair Brush
Coin Purse
Glasses
Headband
Neckerchief
Barrette
Umbrella
Ribbon
Wallet

Fruits

Everybody loves fruits. They are so juicy and delicious.

Watermelon
Plum
Fig
Kiwi
Guava
Mango
Lemon
Pomegranate
Apricot
Papaya

Vegetables

Vegetables are good for health.
You should eat your vegetables.

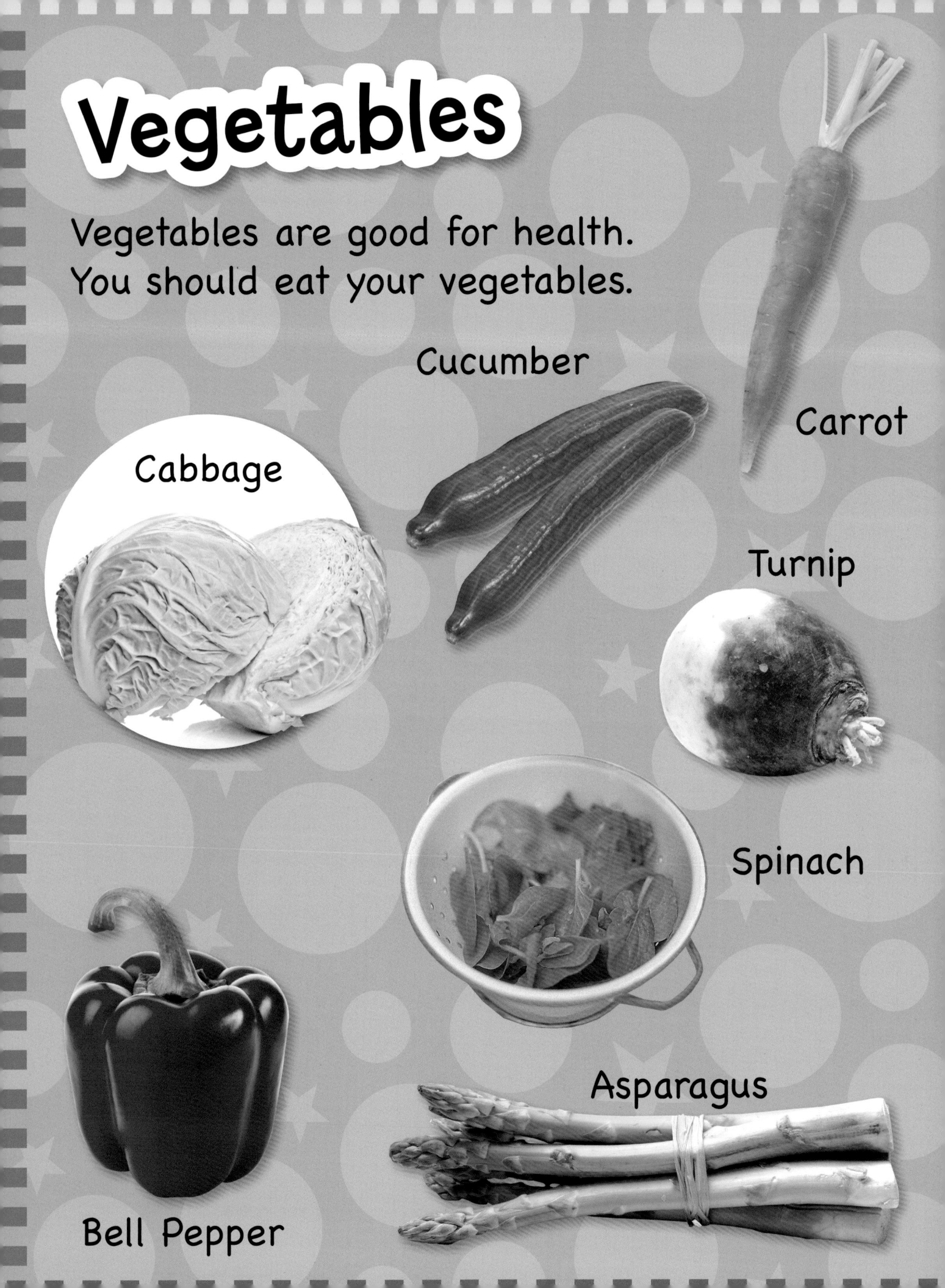

Celery
Broccoli
Radish
Peas
Lettuce
Cauliflower
Beetroot
Onion
Potato

Spices We Use

Food tastes good when we add spices to give it flavor.

Star Anise

Coriander

Paprika

Cardamom

Cloves

Fennel

Mint

Oregano
Salt
Ginger
Bay Leaves
Sage
Garlic
Nutmeg
Black Pepper
Saffron
Parsley

Sweets We Eat

Do you have a sweet tooth? Then you will love these sweets.

Fruit Tart
Sweet Butter Fudge
Custard
Jelly Beans
Macarons
Brownie
Swiss Roll
Chocolate Chip Cookies
Sweets
Cream Puffs

Drinks

What do you like to drink on a hot day? Do you like these drinks?

Cola

Cranberry Juice

Buttermilk

Apple Juice

Iced Coffee

Water

Smoothie

Lemonade
Ginger Ale
Orange Juice
Carrot Juice
Tomato Juice
Milk Shake
Coffee
Hot Chocolate
Tea
Iced Tea

Foods We Eat

What is your favorite food?
Do you like any of these?

Sushi

Fajita

Pasta

Cheeseburger

Soup

Corn-on-the-Cob

Meatloaf

Pancakes

Lasagna
Taco
Salad
Fish and Chips
Bacon Roll
Curry
Pizza
Fried Rice
Steak

Snacks

Feeling hungry? How about a tasty snack?

Bagel

Chips

Croissant

Crackers

Energy Bar

Doughnuts

Hot Dog

Sandwich

Nachos
Pretzel
Nuts
Quiche
Waffles
Marshmallows
Raisins
Wafers
Popcorn
Popcorn

Condiments

These products help make our food taste better. Ketchup, anyone?

Jam
Chilli Sauce
Mustard
Chocolate Sauce
Marmalade
Sour Cream
Mayonnaise
Barbeque Sauce
Cheese Spread
Salsa

Flowers

Everybody loves flowers. They are so colorful and sweet smelling.

Lotus

Rose

Forget-Me-Not

Foxglove

Chrysanthemum

Lily

Sunflower

Tulip
Daffodil
Primrose
Orchid
Bird of Paradise
Iris
Dahlia
Crocus
Daisy

People We Meet

How many of these people have you met lately?

Blacksmith

Doctor

Fisherman

Cobbler

Carpenter

Fireman

Engineer

Farmer
Astronaut
Hair Dresser
Doorman
Chef
Bellboy
Butler
Grocery clerk
Chauffeur

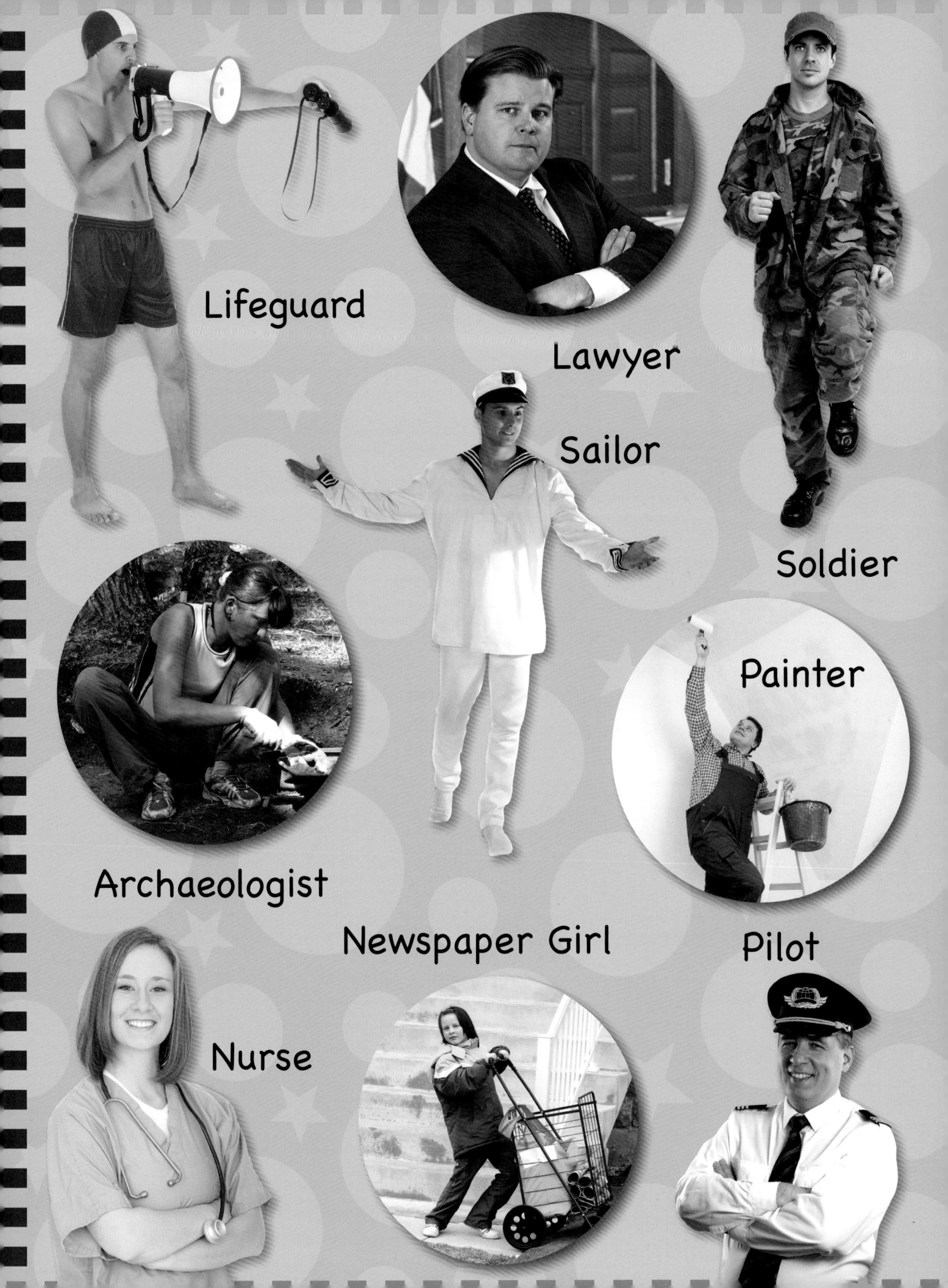
Lifeguard
Lawyer
Sailor
Soldier
Archaeologist
Painter
Newspaper Girl
Pilot
Nurse

Tailor
Postman
Sculptor
Maid
Electrician
Security Guard
Builder
Vet
Beautician

Places We Go

These are some of the places you may visit for different reasons.

Cinema

Amusement Park

Mall

School

Bookshop

Supermarket

Library

Restaurant
Delicatessen
Swimming Pool
Park
Arcade
Laundromat
Zoo
Museum
Clothes Store
Toy Store

Story Characters

What are your favorite characters? What do you like reading about?

Castle

Magician

Prince

King

Princess

Monster

Dragon

Mermaid
Wizard
Troll
Unicorn
Pony
Fairy
Ballerina
Knight
Cowboy

Things to Do

How many of these activities do you do?

Play Fight
Whisper
Sing
Kick
Kiss
Walk
Wave
Stand
Push

My Tools

These are some of the tools your parents might use around the house.

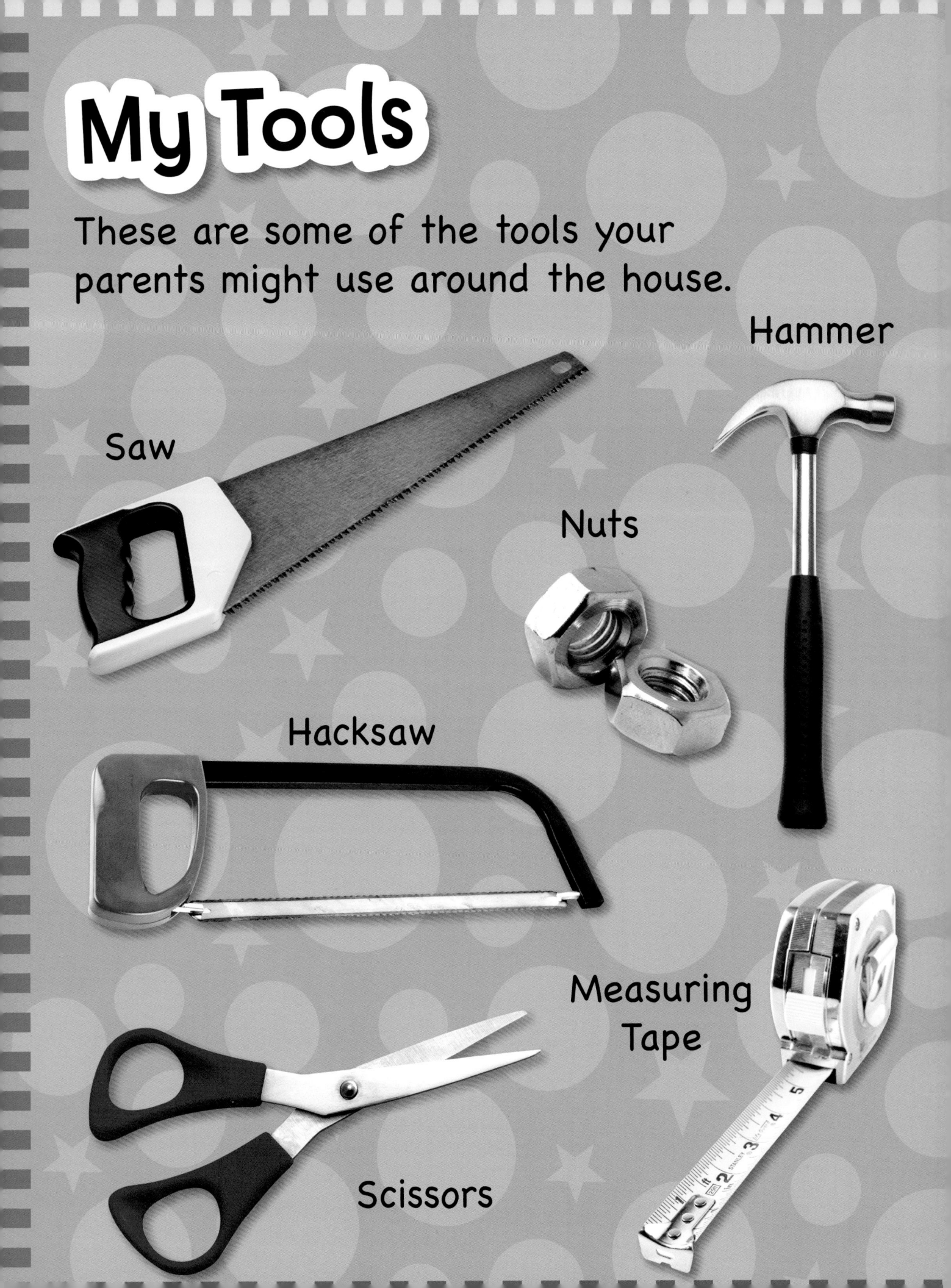

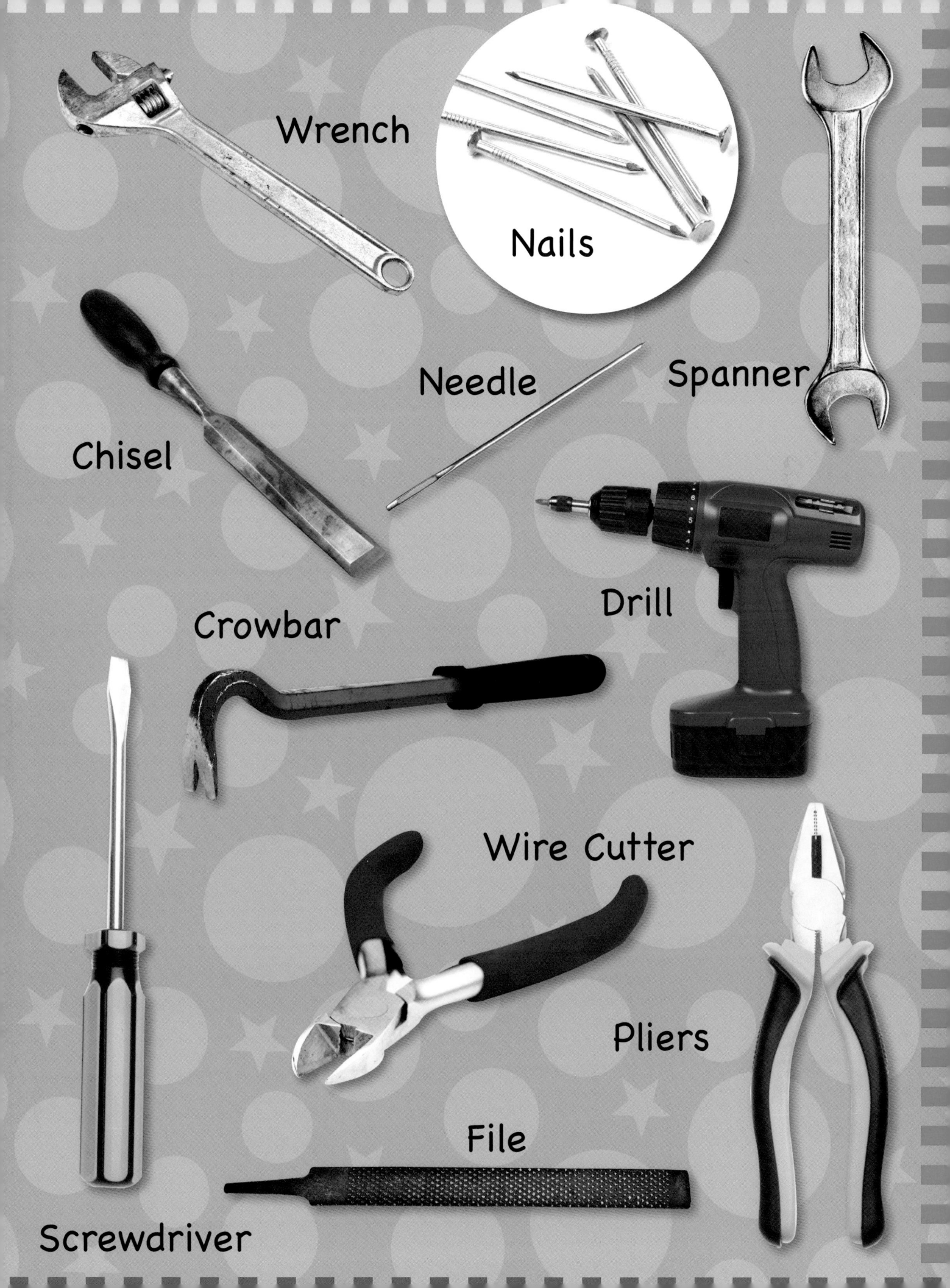
Wrench
Nails
Spanner
Needle
Chisel
Drill
Crowbar
Wire Cutter
Pliers
File
Screwdriver

Baby Animals

What do you think these baby animals will grow up to be?

Kid
Puppy
Lion Cub
Calf
Fawn
Lamb
Tadpole
Alligator Hatchling
Rabbit Kit
Gosling

Valuables

All these things are precious and expensive. Be careful with them.

Amber
Dollar Bills
Platinum
Silver
Diamond
Turquoise
Ruby
Jade
Topaz
Sapphire

Jewelry

Lots of people wear jewelry.

Amulet
Bracelet
Brooch
Hair Pin
Bangle
Hair Sticks
Toe Ring
Ring
Choker

Shapes

These are some of the common shapes you will find around you.

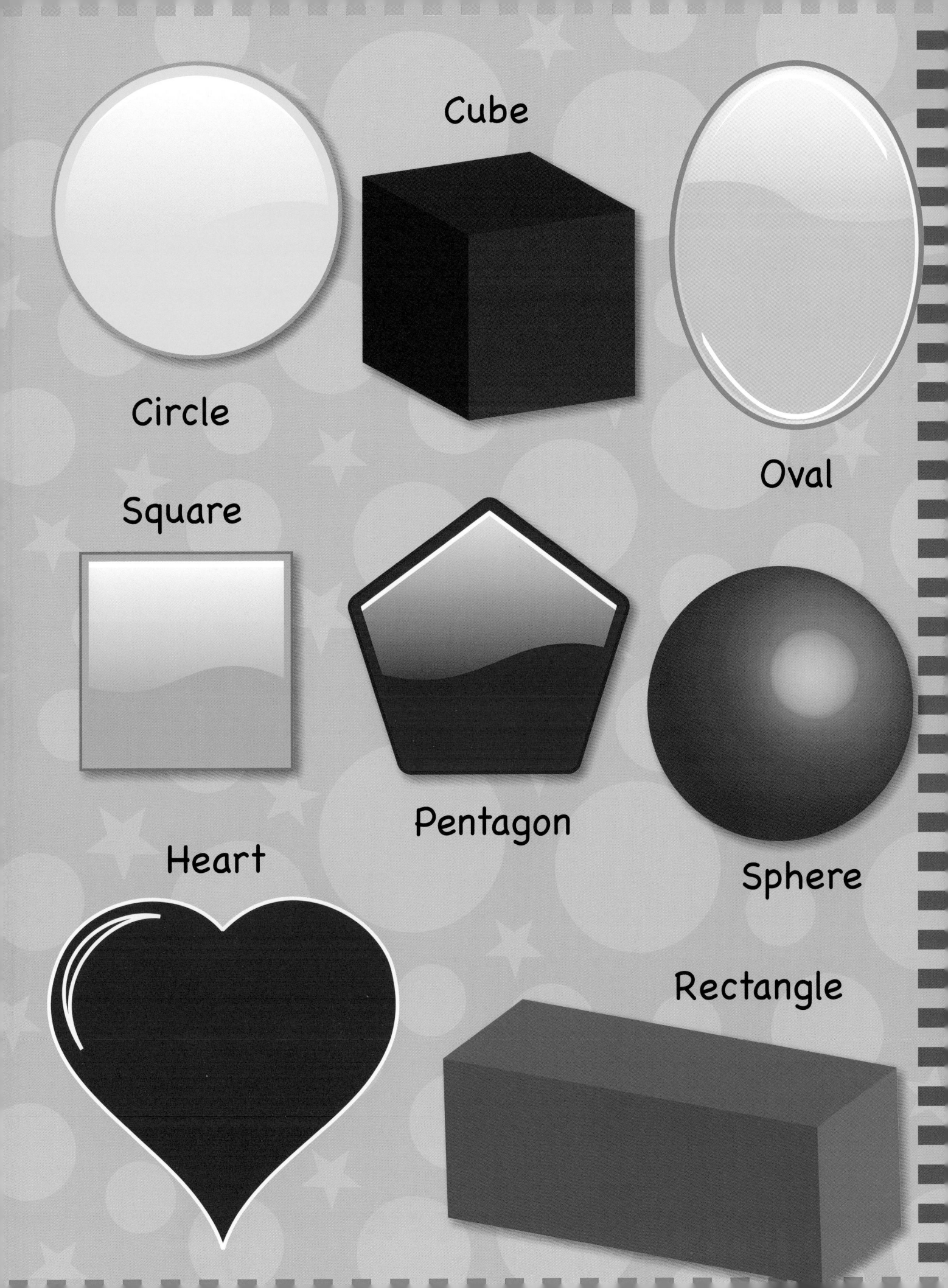
Circle
Cube
Oval
Square
Pentagon
Sphere
Heart
Rectangle